PAPER SOLDIERS OF NAPOLEONIC ERA -3

RUSSIA & HOLLAND
UNIFORMS FROM THE
VINKHUIJZEN COLLECTION

SERIES EDITED BY

Luca Stefano Cristini

SOLDIERSHOP
PUBLISHING
BOOK on DEMAND

PAPER SOLDIERS SERIES

La collana è dedicata alla storia e alla collezione de mitici soldatini di carta o ai soldatini da wargame. In ogni volume preziose raccolte di soldatini stampati il secolo scorso (e anche prima), provenienti dalle nostre collezioni, ma anche nuovi figurini realizzati con abile maestria dai nostri bravi autori. Sempre con l'intento di fornirvi illustrazioni di grande qualità.

RINGRAZIAMENTI E CREDITI FOTOGRAFICI - PHOTOGRAPHIC CREDITS:

Le tavole sono generalmente opera dell'autore o dell'illustratore indicato. La gran parte del resto dell'iconografia usata appartiene all'archivio dell'editore, foto scattate dall'autore, o materiale di amici collezionisti. L'Editore rimane in ogni caso a disposizione degli eventuali aventi diritto per tutte le fonti iconografiche dubbie o non identificate.

Title: **PAPER SOLDIERS OF NAPOLEONIC ERA - 3**
Serie edit by Luca S. Cristini. First edition by Soldiershop. December 2019
Cover & Art Design: Luca S. Cristini. ISBN code: 978-88-93275378
Published by Luca Cristini Editore, via Orio 35/4- 24050 Zanica (BG) ITALY. www.soldiershop.com

PAPER SOLDIERS OF NAPOLEONIC ERA - 3

RUSSIA & HOLLAND FROM THE VINKHUIJZEN COLLECTION

SERIES EDITED BY
LUCA STEFANO CRISTINI

THE VINKHUIJZEN COLLECTION

This famous Collection of Military Costume Illustration consists of over 32,000 diverse pictures from varied sources of costumes mounted in 762 scrapbooks. Elaborate 19th-century European uniforms are the collection's special strength. The aesthetic quality of the images varies, as the collection includes 17th-century festival book prints, 19th-century chromolithographs, original watercolor compositions, pencil drawings, and photographs. Most are plates extracted from illustrated books and magazines.

all the pictures are organized by country and time period. The many scrapbooks devoted to Germany and Italy include separate designations for pre-unification states and principalities.

Assembled by one of these great, eccentric collectors of the late 19th Century, Dr. Hendrik Jacobus Vinkhuijzen, a Dutch medical doctor.

Dr. Vinkhuijzen traveled throughout Europe as a physician associated with various armies and with the Dutch royal court for. He began his career as a medical officer with the Royal Sharpshooters Corps in The Hague. During the Franco-Prussian War he served in France on an ambulance with the newly founded Red Cross. He also traveled to Russia, where he stayed in Moscow studying "the fight against pestilence." In his later life, he was the official court physician to Prince Alexander of the Netherlands. His father had performed in the same role for King Willem III.

ITALIAN TEXT

LA COLLEZIONE VINKHUIJZEN

Collezionista eccentrico e appassionato cultore di iconografia militare era un contemporaneo del famoso uniformologo Quinto Cenni, visse infatti fra il 1840 e il 1910., il Dr. H. J. Vinkhuijzen, iniziò la sua carriera come medico dell'esercito olandese fino a diventare medico ufficiale di corte del principe Alessandro dei Paesi Bassi. La sua vasta collezione arrivò a contare oltre 32.000 soggetti. Moltissimi e pressoché sconosciuti fino alla loro pubblicazione nella nostra collana Quaderni Cenni, quelli realizzati espressamente per la sua collezione da parte del pittore emiliano. Dal 1911 la collezione è stata donata alla New York Public Library dal sig. Henry Draper erede del medico olandese. Ed è da questa collezione che Soldiershop prende i soggetti di questa nuova pubblicazione di soldatini di carta. Ogni immagine ha subito una rigorosa pulizia e ri-classificazione per fornire agli appassionati di storia militare e costume un'opera completa, agevole e utile per tutti gli studiosi e gli appassionati di uniformologia e non solo.

THE PLATES
OF RUSSIAN ARMY

Russia infantry 1813-15

Russia infantry chasseur and musketeer (below) 1813

Russia Guard infantry voltigeur and fusilier (below) 1813

Russia Guard infantry grenadier and Preobraženskij (below) 1813

Russia Guard infantry Preobraženskij and regimental band 1813

Russia Guard infantry Preobraženskij and regimental band 1813

Russia landwehr infantry 1813-1815

Russia landwehr infantry 1813-1815

Russian generals staff 1813-1815

Russia artillery man 1813-1815

Russia artillery 1813-1815

Russia dragoons cavalry regiment 1813-1815 - below irregular cavalry Bashir 1813

Bashkiren

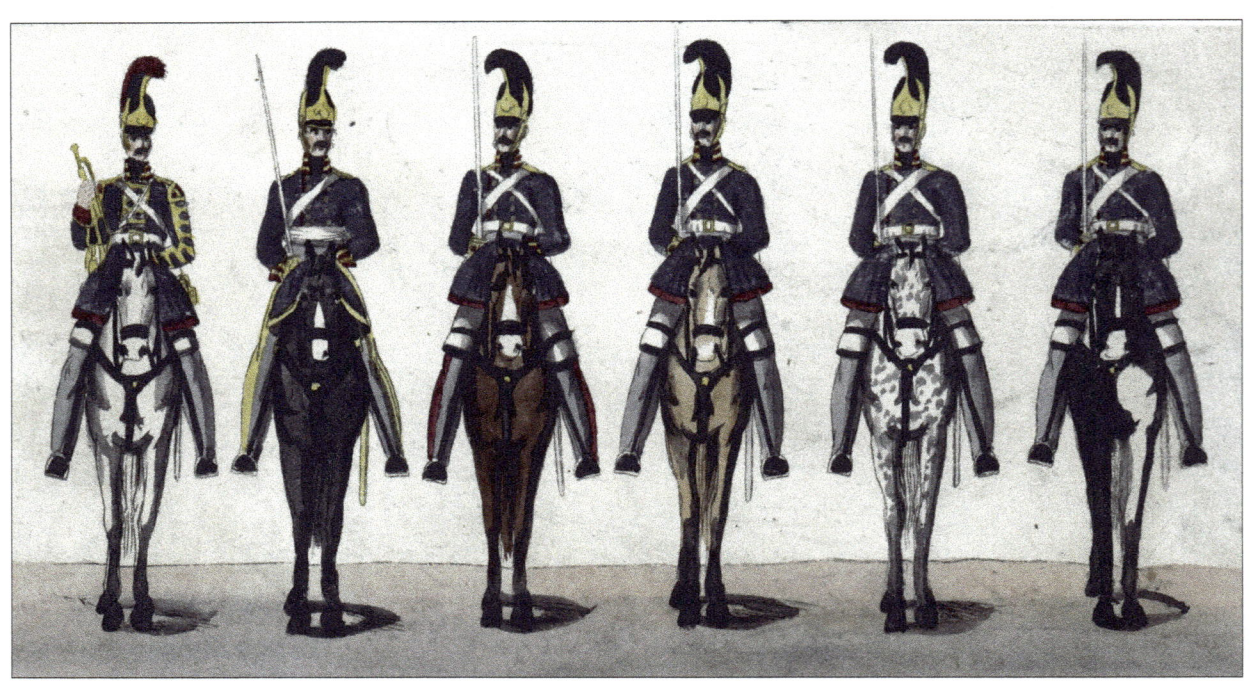

Russia dragoons cavalry regiment 1813-1815 - below irregular cavalry Bashir 1813

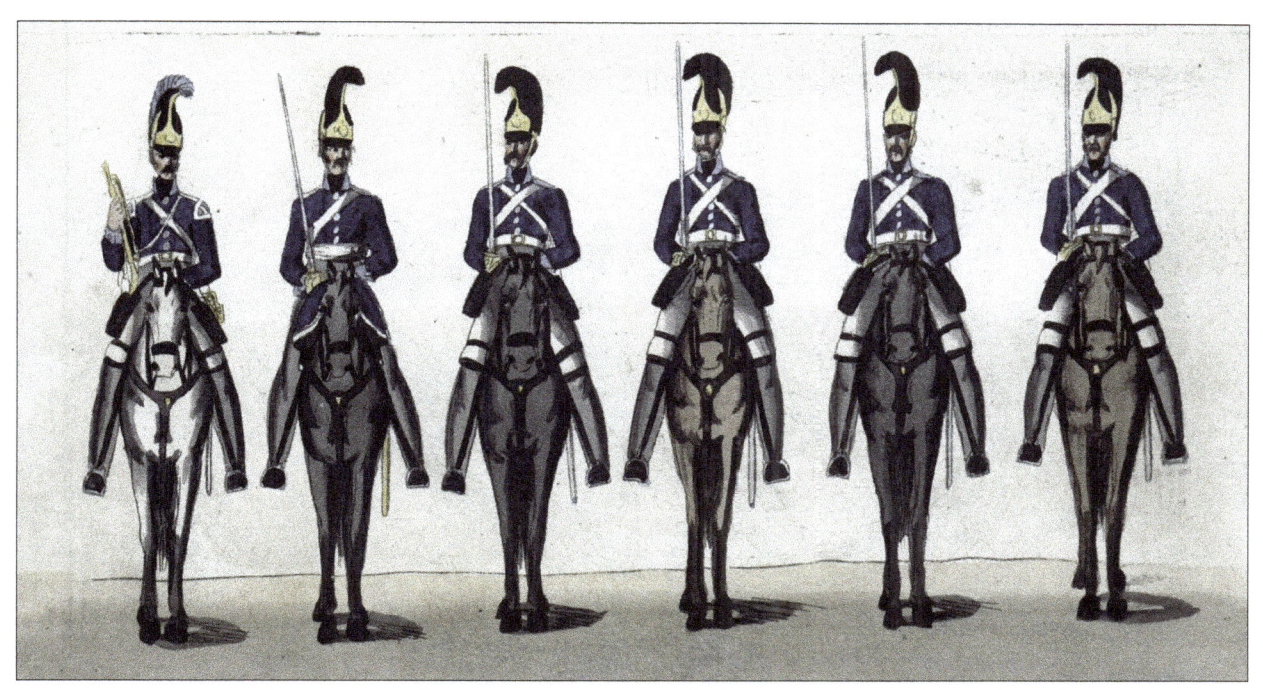

Russia dragoons cavalry regiment 1813-1815 - below irregular cavalry Bashir 1813

Russia dragoons cavalry regiment 1813-1815 - below irregular cavalry Bashir 1813

Russia Guard Cuirassier cavalry regiment 1813-1815 - below irregular cavalry Kalmuch 1813-1814

Kalmäcken
1813 - 1814

Russia Cuirassier cavalry regiment 1813-1815 - below irregular cavalry Kalmuch 1813-1814

Kalmücken
1813

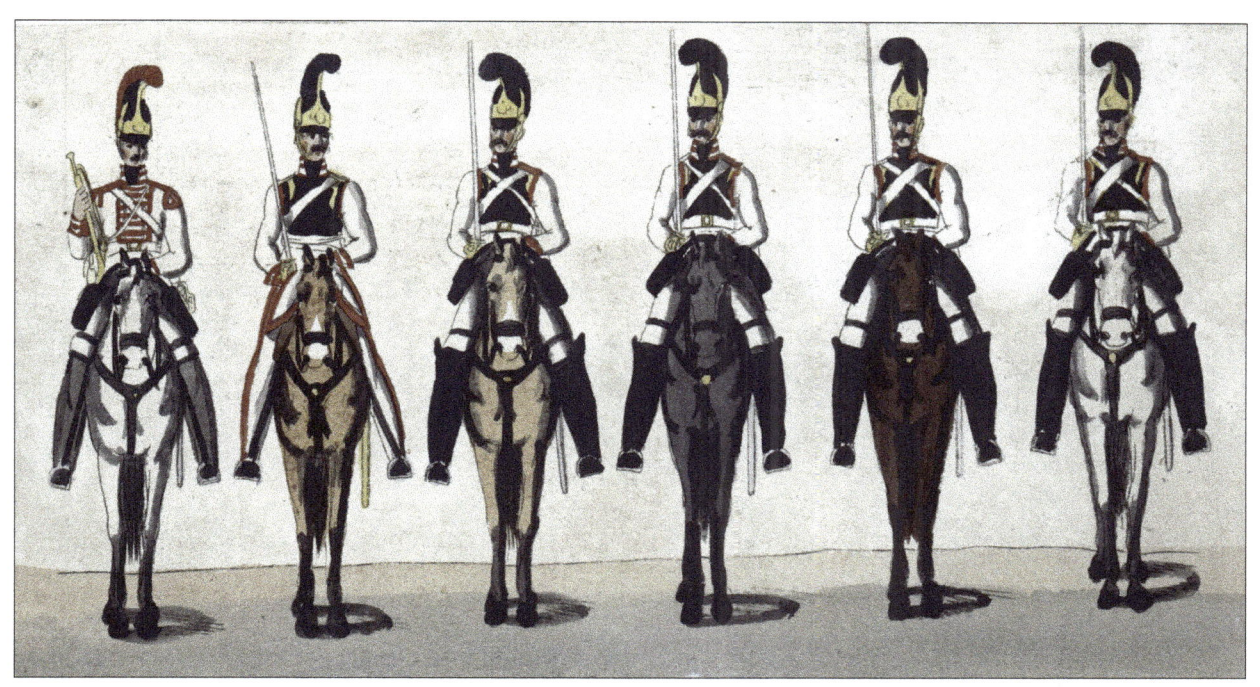

Russia Cuirassier cavalry regiment 1813-1815 - below irregular cavalry Caucasian 1813-1814

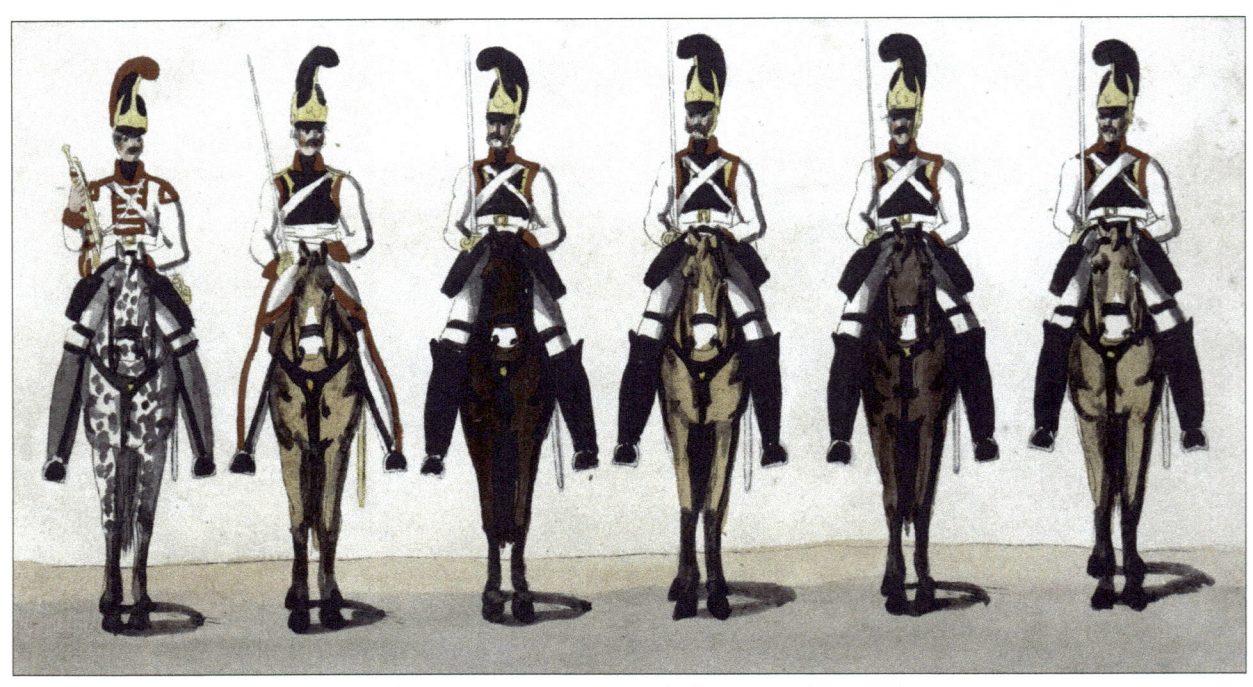

Russia Cuirassier cavalry regiment 1813-1815 - below irregular cavalry Kirgisi 1813-1814

Kirgisen

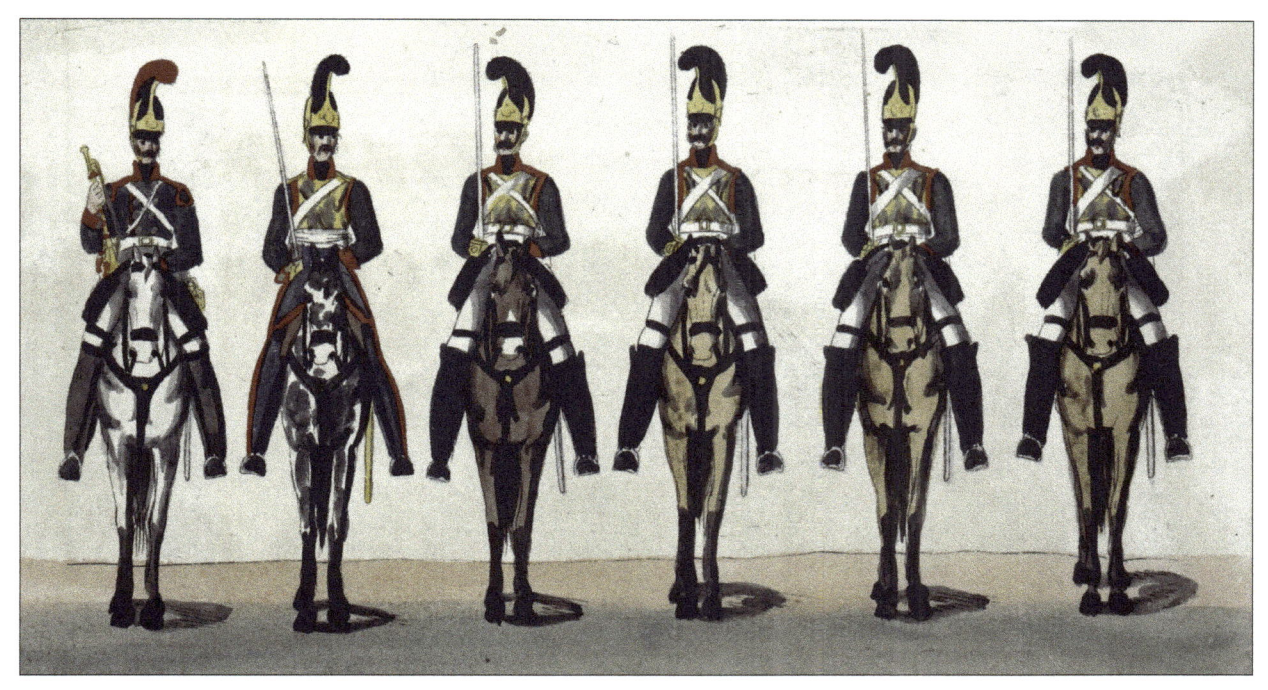

Russia Cuirassier cavalry regiment 1813-1815 - below irregular cavalry Tartars 1813-1814

Tartaren

Russia Hulan cavalry regiment 1813-1815

Russia Hulan cavalry regiment 1813-1815

Russia Hulan cavalry regiment 1813-1815

Russia Cossacks cavalry Bauer regiment 1813-1815

Russia Guard Cossacks cavalry regiment 1813-1815

Russia Guard Cossacks cavalry regiment 1813-1815

Russia Irregular Cossacks cavalry 1813-1815

Russia Cossacks cavalry regiment 1813-1815

Russia Hussar cavalry regiment 1813-1815

Russia Hussar cavalry regiment 1813-1815

Russia Hussar cavalry regiment 1813-1815

Russia Hussar cavalry regiment 1813-1815

Russia Hussar cavalry regiment 1813-1815

Russia Hussar cavalry regiment 1813-1815

Russia Hussar of the death cavalry regiment 1813-1815

THE PLATES
OF DUTCH ARMY

1810 Holland *chasseur* of the Guard

1810 Holland grenadier of the Guard

1810 Holland 3th line regiment - voltigeurs

1810 Holland 3th line regiment

1810 Holland artillery regiment

1810 Holland 5th line regiment below line regiment

1810 Holland cavalry regiment

PAPER SOLDIERS ALREADY PUBLISHED & IN WORKING

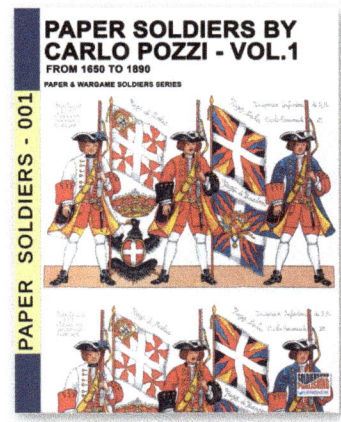

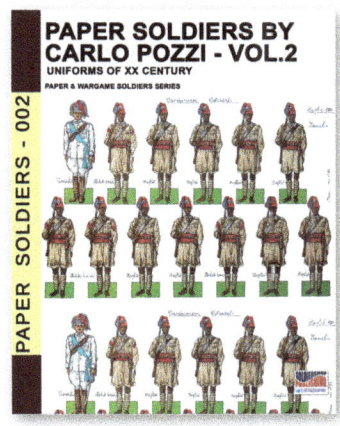

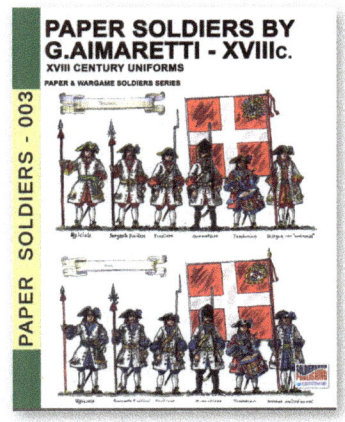

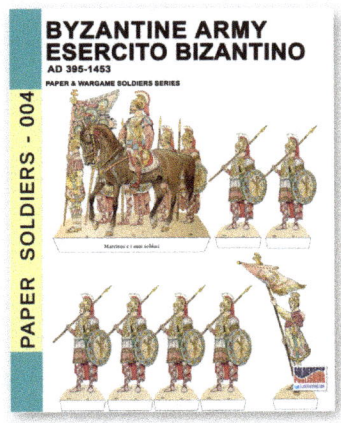

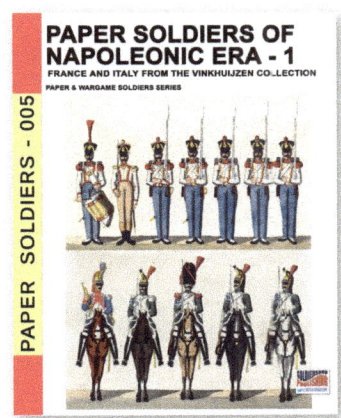

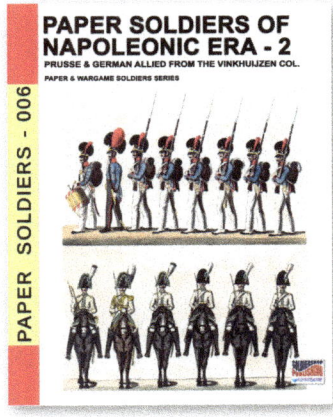

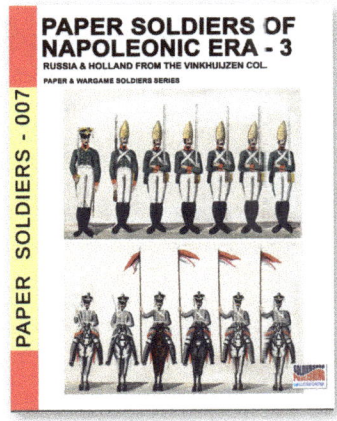